HAL•LEONARD
INSTRUMENTAL PLAY-ALONG

AUDIO ACCESS INCLUDED

POPULAR Hits

To access audio visit:
www.halleonard.com/mylibrary

Enter Code
4155-0911-9130-3754

ISBN 978-1-4234-9998-5

HAL•LEONARD® CORPORATION
7777 W. BLUEMOUND RD. P.O. BOX 13819 MILWAUKEE, WI 53213

Visit Hal Leonard Online at
www.halleonard.com

BREAKEVEN

ALTO SAX

Words and Music by STEPHEN KIPNER, ANDREW FRAMPTON,
DANIEL O'DONOGHUE and MARK SHEEHAN

THE CLIMB

from HANNAH MONTANA: THE MOVIE

ALTO SAX

Words and Music by
JESSI ALEXANDER and JON MABE

FALLIN' FOR YOU

ALTO SAX

Words and Music by
COLBIE CAILLAT and RICK NOWELS

FIREFLIES

ALTO SAX

Words and Music by
ADAM YOUNG

HALO

ALTO SAX

Words and Music by BEYONCÉ KNOWLES,
RYAN TEDDER and EVAN BOGART

HEY, SOUL SISTER

ALTO SAX

Words and Music by PAT MONAHAN,
ESPEN LIND and AMUND BJORKLAND

I GOTTA FEELING

Words and Music by WILL ADAMS,
ALLAN PINEDA, JAIME GOMEZ, STACY FERGUSON,
DAVID GUETTA and FREDERIC RIESTERER

ALTO SAX

I'M YOURS

ALTO SAX

Words and Music by
JASON MRAZ

LOVE STORY

ALTO SAX

Words and Music by
TAYLOR SWIFT

NEED YOU NOW

ALTO SAX

Words and Music by HILLARY SCOTT,
CHARLES KELLEY, DAVE HAYWOOD and JOSH KEAR

POKER FACE

Words and Music by
STEFANI GERMANOTTA and REDONE

ALTO SAX

SMILE

ALTO SAX

Words and Music by BLAIR DALY, JEREMY BOSE,
MATTHEW SHAFER and JOHN HARDING

VIVA LA VIDA

ALTO SAX

Words and Music by GUY BERRYMAN,
JON BUCKLAND, WILL CHAMPION and CHRIS MARTIN

YOU BELONG WITH ME

ALTO SAX

Words and Music by
TAYLOR SWIFT and LIZ ROSE

Moderate Rock

USE SOMEBODY

ALTO SAX

Words and Music by CALEB FOLLOWILL, NATHAN FOLLOWILL,
JARED FOLLOWILL and MATTHEW FOLLOWILL